REVISED AND UPDATED EDITION

CPA SECRETS

UNDERGROUND PLAYBOOK

ATING CAMPAIGNS THAT GENERATE FAST CONVERSATIONS
AND PROFITS WITH EASE THAT CAN BE SCALED UP

AYOL HOPE

Disclaimer

This e-book has been written for information purposes only. Every effort has been made to make this ebook as complete and accurate as possible. However, there may be mistakes in typography or content. Also, this ebook provides information only up to the publishing date. Therefore, this ebook should be used as a guide - not as the ultimate source. The purpose of this ebook is to educate. The author and the publisher does not warrant that the information contained in this e-book is fully complete and shall not be responsible for any errors or omissions. The author and publisher shall have neither liability nor responsibility to any person or entity with respect to any loss or damage caused or alleged to be caused directly or indirectly by this ebook.

KAYOL R. HOPE

Helping small business owners find,
connect, and gain new paying customers
from the web.
Visit: www.kayolhope.com

WHAT'S INSIDE...

RANK WITH SEO AND PROFIT FROM CPA

JOINING CONTENT LOCKING NETWORKS

HOW TO APPLY TO CPA NETWORKS?

CREATING CONTENT/FILES & LOCK DOCUMENTS

RANK WITH SEO AND PROFIT FROM CPA

Today I'll show you a simple CPA *(Cost Per Action)* method that uses innovative traffic sources and combines SEO *(Search Engine Optimization)* to setup an optimal campaign with dead simple tracking for maximum CPA conversions that generate profitable commissions in red-hot niches in under a week.

CPA marketing is popular widely and used in order to earn fast cash or a steady income through various online business opportunities and marketing platforms. Using YouTube as a *"free"* traffic source you can drive traffic along with *content lockers* to monetize the incentive offers. Not only are videos much easier to create than long-winded articles, they're also consumed with a higher retention rate.

Basically through a content locking CPA network, you can upload mostly anything you want *(no porn, child abuse or wifi hack)* and then you promote your content or files online.

Your locked content can be in the form of ebook, software, document, video, etc. and even your web content or links.

The catch is that the person that want to view or download your content/file, will have to complete a small survey or offer or to download and install a promotional software, in order to get access to it.

Usually the content will be unblocked immediately and will be blocked again after few minutes or few days depend on the setting or the lockers from each different network. The user's IP address will be used to determine the number of time he or she has accessed to the links or files and such the permission for him or her to gain access them.

The amount you get per survey completed differs from survey to survey and it typically ranges between $0.11 to $20 on average.

Surveys differ from country to country. The bottom thing is that the more views/downloads you generate, the more money you make.

Although, here I mention the YouTube method ONLY for driving traffic because it is the most effective way to promote this type of CPA you can easily scale this method by driving traffic through torrent sites, websites and/or blog, forums, and other social media networks.

JOINING CONTENT LOCKING NETWORKS

There are tons of CPA networks which offer content locking and some of them are pure 100% content locking networks. If you haven't join any CPA networks before, I recommend that you join at least one of the following networks that we highly recommend you to join:

AdscendMedia:
http://kayolhope.com/adscendmedia/
CPALead   (Instant   Approval):
http://kayolhope.com/cpalead/
Fileice: http://fileice.net/

NOTE: Instant approval still requires you to have a website/blog which are running by yourself in order to get into these networks easier.

I highly recommend you to register a domain - http://kayolhope.com/hostgator *(You should choose a domain name related to your niche)* and get a website hosted if you haven't done so, this is NECESSARY as you must host your own files in some of the locking content networks, furthermore, you CANNOT get your Youtube Annotation link and WordPress redirect plug-in works without your own website.

And having your own website has the advantages of using one of the approaches of keyword research and embed your video to others web properties.

And having your own website has the advantages of using one of the approaches of keyword research and embed your video to others web properties.

HOW TO APPLY TO CPA NETWORKS?

Be honest!

If you are honest to them, they will approve you. Here are our tips to get approved without problems:

* Only valid data *(like your name, address, etc.)*

* Try to apply with a business email address *(so, everything expect a Gmail or Yahoo! address or any other free hosting provider)*

For the *"Experience"*

Question?, answer it like that: If you don't have experience at all in this kind of business:

Ii, my name is [Your Name]. I'm pretty new in this

m willing to work and improve my knowledge on

ing up a lot about CPA in the past and would be g

ethod with Paid traffic, which I want to apply with

k. If for any reason you need to contact me, feel f

want.

CREATING CONTENT/FILES & LOCK DOCUMENTS

Bear in mind that when choosing a niche you must always consider the most profitable one but you cannot avoid measuring their competitiveness as well.

Once you have chosen your niche, you can prepare the offer such as a ebook, course, software, etc. that visitors can download once they are interested in the content that you provide.

Of course you can compile your unique ebook/files if you have some knowledge of the subject of the niche. But you can also download some free or paid PLR *(Private Label Rights)* or MRR *(Master Resell Rights)* products as long as make sure the file that you're going to download has *"Giveaway Rights Included"*, if you are unsure please contact the product owner for clarification.

The most important thing to remember is to make sure the content being rewarded is of good value. If you provide junk than you'll be labeled a spammer and fail to profit.

UPLOAD FILES/EBOOKS

Before uploading the file that you obtained, it is advised to split the ebook, video or audio into 2 parts to become two separated files of Part 1 and 2. Doing this you will need any free PDF software for ebook, which you can search in the Internet.

For video and audio files, we recommend you using *ScreenFlow*, which has an awesome splitting feature build-in.

A bit of an investment however, the learning curve is fairly easy and quality of my videos always come out looking professional. After comparing other similar competitor solutions of the same caliber I've found ScreenFlow to be hands down the best Screen recording, Screencasting, and video editing software for Mac.

ScreenFlow by Telestream:
http://kayolhope.com/screenflow/

If unfortunately you cannot do this, you
can just simply search and download
another file that has a similar or
related content with your first file.

The reason to have two separated files
is because you are going to upload
these to two different networks to
maximize your profit.

After splitting the file into 2 parts, just compress *(zip)* it with another text file *(Often the use of txt documents with a link for Part 2)* or related content file for your visitor to download. And again, of course the file will be locked.

Finished, now your zipped file is ready for uploading!

VIDEO CREATING AND UPLOADING

You can produce your video simply using Slide Show with some free or paid tools, but what I advise is that you use real people for demonstration in the video since it is the most effective way to attract view in YouTube.

I'm not going to discuss making videos using various tools because you can simply find many tutorials in the Internet. If you would like to spend more time to learn about other tools and editors, please see the *Free Resources section*.

Resources Section:
http://kayolhope.com/resources

What I'm going to discuss are only 2 approaches for creating a quality video.

First one is by capturing yourself through YouTube feature if you are comfortable for speaking in front of camera. The second approach is by hiring some experts for the video demonstration.

You video should not be longer than an average song clip, preferably below 4 minutes, *(in order not to lose viewers' attention)*. Make it simple, with clear messages and call to action.

2 KINDS of videos that are easier to get view and traffic:

INSTRUCTION-DEMONSTRATION-HOW TO

These videos are usually longer and more detailed. Google love them and they are often rank higher and included on Google top pages. If you make a short video it is a good idea to start with questions related to the problem followed by the main benefit points *("How To" solve the problem and answers to the questions)* and finally a clear call to action *(for example: click on the link below).*

TESTIMONIALS

These videos are usually used in addition to your main marketing video and represent live recording of a person who is using or have used the product.

Therefore someone other than you can only do this approach. The fastest approach is to hire someone to give you a positive testimonial after giving him the product for a review.

Try to identify keywords with at least 1,000 searches per month and with less than 50,000 competitor pages for the *"Phrase"* option. If you go after these types of keywords it will greatly increase the chances to get your video on the first page of Google.

I would also like to address here the approach of finding so- called video retainer keywords. The idea is to type keyword candidates into Google and see if there are videos on pages 1-3 of the Google results. If videos are there then you are likely to rank your video on one of the first Google pages too. Conversely, if there are no videos then you should avoid such keywords.

Taking into account my own experiences and the fact that Google's algorithm always changes, my opinion is that it is often not the case. Therefore, while I agree that this is a valuable strategy I personally do not make it as one of the most important considerations.

Tip: Keywords starting with *"How To"* are very good candidates for ranking videos on Google.

If you do not have your own website and have a long affiliate link, you should use URL shortening services like bit.ly. It shortens and cloaks the ugly looking link and, what is important, provides tracking data. But this make possible for your video been stroked by YouTube review team. If you do have your own website with WordPress installed, use a WordPress plugin which can shorten your CPA network's link. This is a safer way to make your link.

Note: A direct link to CPA offer/download file is impossible to integrate into the annotation and card since YouTube only allow associated website, i.e. your website link. Therefore using a re-direct plugin is a must!

In conclusion, I would like to say that obviously there are better ways, tools and methods to make money with CPA content locking, I hope this provides enough free/paid and (semi)-automated tools and resources for you to get started and quickly get your videos ranked on YouTube and make some passive income via CPA content locking. Take action and good luck!

Need further assistance with optimizing your video(s)? I'm an SEO Experts and can help you by providing link building services and social signals to your CPA offers.

Services:

http://kayolhope.com/services